MICHIGAN MOVIE THEATRES

A Pictorial History

Michael V. Doyle

Michigan Movie Theatres: A Pictorial History © 2003 by Michael V. Doyle

All rights reserved under International and Pan American Copyright Conventions. No part of this book may be reproduced in any manner whatsoever without written permission from the author, except in the case of brief quotations embodied in reviews and articles.

Printed in the United States of America

08 07 06 05 04 03   5 4 3 2 1

ISBN 0-9677570-2-9

Cover and text design by Michael Smith/View Two Plus

Boreal Press

Haslett, Michigan

Table of Contents

Introduction iv
Author's Reflections vi
The Founding Fathers of Michigan's Theatre Industry 1
    A Chronology of Walter S. Butterfield Theatres, Inc. 2
    Colonel Walter Scott Butterfield 3
    Reflections of a Butterfield Theatres Manager 8
    William "Emmett" Goodrich 11
    Jack Loeks Theatres 14
    The Poisson Dynasty 17
The Evolution of the Movie Palace 21
    A Brief History of Movie Theatres in the United States .. 22
    Movie Theatre Architecture 27
Movie Theatre Advertising 37
Theatre Gallery
    Lower Peninsula Theatres 47
    Upper Peninsula Theatres 119
Other Theatres 127
Photography Credits 131
Selected Bibliography 133
Index 135
About the Author 136

Introduction

This book profiles first- and second-run movie theatres in Michigan, as determined by the author. Every effort has been made to show representative photos of the theatres when they were still in operation. Most photos depict the theatre as it was known in the 1930s, 40s or 50s. The author acknowledges many of these movie houses changed names over the years of their operation, sometimes two or three times; however, the photos reflect the theatre in its most stable operation. Every effort was made to include the date the movie theatre opened; however, some records are incomplete since many movie houses were converted to other businesses, parking lots, or left as vacant properties. Therefore, where the date the theatre was built is indicated in the text, it may actually reflect the decade that the building was erected.

A word about editorial license. I have decided to use the spelling "theatre," which is the British derivation. This is the common spelling of the word used by most movie chains through the 1950s. On the pages dedicated to photographs and histories of movie theatres, those theatres that have several names are printed in the order of most recent name first.

A good deal of attention will be given to the Butterfield Theatres, Inc., which owned and operated most of the outstate first- and second-run theatres and drive-ins in Michigan.

Movie promotion and advertising was a great part of the theatre business. I have included representative newspaper advertisements of the period for readers to sample. Because I spent my childhood and teenage years in Grand Rapids, I have included detailed recollections of theatres in this city, including a long, comprehensive list, as well as in Lansing, where I spent my professional career. A comprehensive list of Grand Rapids theatres is included in this section to highlight the scope of the movie business in a major Michigan city. Detailed biographies are provided of independent theatre owners Jack Loeks (Midtown), William "Emmett" Goodrich (Savoy), and the Poisson family (Eastown, Four-Star, Wealthy, and Royal), whose lives enriched the theatre business in Grand Rapids in its formative years. A detailed biography of theatre owner Colonel Walter S. Butterfield, who founded and managed most of the major outstate movie houses, is also included. An interview with long-time Butterfield city manager Earl Barry of Flint gives insight into what a theatre manager's duties represented.

This book would not be complete without a sampling of selected smaller movie theatres in Michigan; therefore I have included a montage of photos for the reader. Finally, a selected bibliography of movie theatre literature is included at the end of the book.

A special thanks to those individuals who helped me in preparing this book: Michael M. Smith for his design of the book; Loretta Crum, publisher and editor; and William S. Davis, research assistant. Thanks also to theatre owners Bob Goodrich, John Loeks, Jr., and Gary Geiger for their insights and information. Special thanks to Joe Sterling of Monroe, Michigan, Butterfield Theatres executive; Michael Hauser, marketing manager, Michigan Opera Theatre; and Earl Berry, former Flint city manager for Butterfield Theatres.

Michael V. Doyle, Ph.D.
East Lansing, Michigan

Author's Reflections

My first reflections of movie theatres was at a very young age, as a boy growing up in my home town of Grand Rapids, Michigan. The downtown theatres—the Majestic, Midtown, Keith's, Regent, and Savoy—are my first memories. It was the neon lights and large posters that drew me to them. I can remember *Quo Vadis* and *Showboat* at the Midtown Theatre. The front of the theatre was designed to incorporate large three-sheet and six-sheet posters, as well as banners, to create an image of excitement for the movies. The same occurred at the Majestic, when it opened the movie, *House of Wax* in 3-D. I was a frequent visitor to the Savoy, with its 40-by-60 inch poster frames and the best marquee in Grand Rapids

The Keith's and the Regent were the grand old theatres in Grand Rapids, still displaying the ornate beauty of the 1920s when vaudeville's Keith-Albee Circuit stars played there. In the 1950s, both theatres were updated to include the more modern 40-by-60 inch posters for display in front underneath the marquee. I also could count on downtown theatres having more lobby cards, stills, and banners for display. My first poster was a lobby card given to me by the Midtown Theatre's caretaker. Who would guess I would have more than a thousand posters in my own collection years later? I also remember the Center and Kent Theatres on Lower Monroe, both close to each other. They generally showed second-run and action pictures in the late 1950s as first-run product became more scarce.

Neighborhood theatres didn't escape my interest. The Eastown was my favorite. Not only did the Eastown have 40-by-60 inch posters in front of the theatre, but for years it also had a hand-painted banner atop the doors as you entered. The Four-

Star, on Division, was a copy of the Eastown's design. Both were B&J Theatres. The Creston, on Plainfield N.E., was my neighborhood theatre. This theatre was owned by Harry Himmelstein, whose son was in my high school class. Although this was a sub-run theatre, the exterior offered complete sets of lobby cards, one-sheets, and two inserts. I also remember the Family Theatre, on Michigan N.E. It had large 40-by-60 inch poster frames in the front and an interesting Egyptian design interior. This was quite unusual for such a small neighborhood theatre.

Reflections of Lansing theatres are a bit more recent. Since I have been in the East Lansing community for over thirty years with Michigan State University, I have observed firsthand the closing of many Lansing theatres. I saw my first Lansing movie theatre as a child when my parents stopped at the old Kewpie Restaurant on Grand River Avenue across from Michigan State. I think this was about 1952, since the movie playing at the Lucon Theatre—later the Campus—was *The Las Vegas Story* starring Jane Russell and Robert Mitchum. The Lucon was a first-run theatre. It was sad to see this theatre, as well as the State on Abbott Road, both destroyed in the 1980s due to urban renewal projects. It is ironic to note that at press time for this book, East Lansing no longer has a downtown movie theatre.

Downtown Lansing was almost void of movie houses by the time I arrived in the area in the 1960s. However, the ornate Michigan and Gladmer theatres were still in operation. The Michigan was the flagship of Lansing's Butterfield Theatre chain. It was also the largest theatre in Lansing. I remember seeing *Grease* in this wonderful movie palace with only about 25 other people in the audience. Both the Michigan and Gladmer had large 40-by-60 inch poster frames and a full set of lobby cards and inserts.

As I look at both the Grand Rapids and Lansing theatre districts today, there is no visible sign of the theatres I knew and loved. In Grand Rapids, urban renewal has taken all the downtown theatres except the Majestic, which remains as the home of the Grand Rapids Civic Players. Lansing's grand Michigan Theatre is now office space and only retains small glimpses of its former grandeur. I miss the lights and marquees the most, because they were a sign of glamour and wonder as they lit up the theatres they framed. Movie posters and large advertisements of the films playing at modern theatres have been streamlined and leave little to the imagination. The changing look of today's movie theatres seems to me to reflect the standardization of society as a whole. Thankfully, I was able to see the movie theatres of Grand Rapids and Lansing in all their splendor before their demise. ∎

The Founding Fathers
of Michigan's Theatre Industry

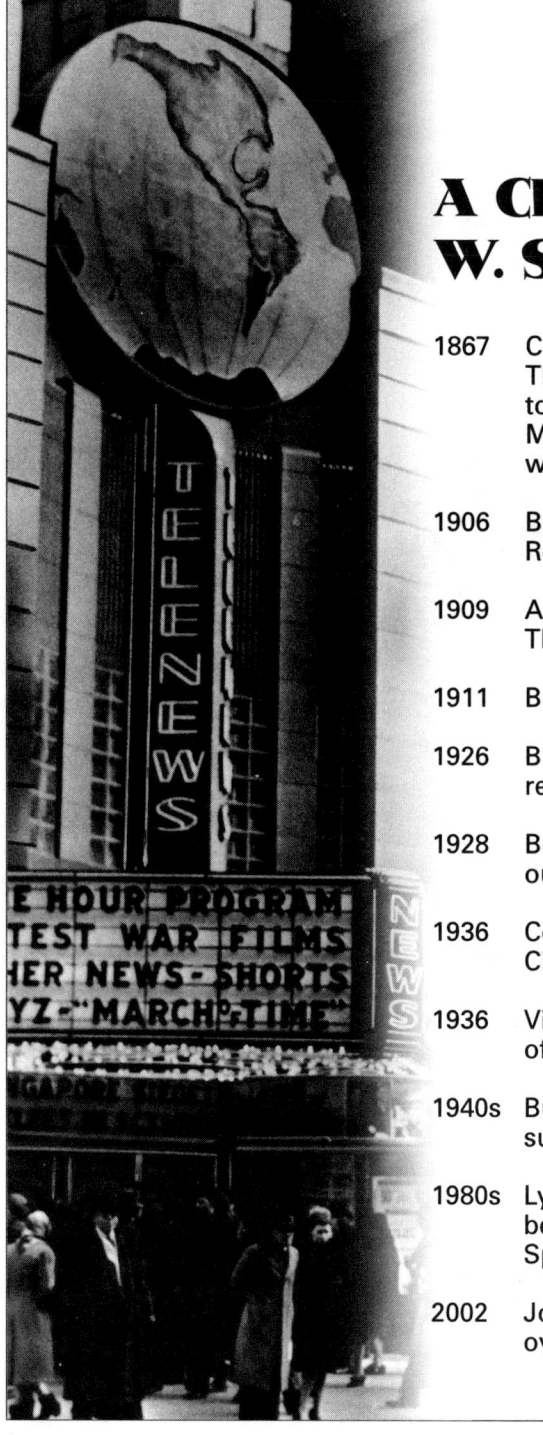

A Chronology of W. S. Butterfield Theatres, Inc.

1867   Colonel Walter Scott Butterfield, founder of Butterfield Theatres, Inc., is born. "Colonel" was an honorary title given to Walter by the troops at Fort Custer in Battle Creek, Michigan, in appreciation of his efforts to provide them with entertainment.

1906   Butterfield purchases Hamblin Opera House in Battle Creek. Renamed as the Bijou, this was his first theatre.

1909   A new building is erected to replace the original Bijou. The new Bijou Theatre opened on September 13, 1909.

1911   Butterfield organizes Bijou Theatre Enterprises, Inc.

1926   Butterfield moves his corporate offices to Detroit in 1926, renaming the company Butterfield Theatre Enterprises, Inc.

1928   Butterfield Theatres is operating 75 theatres in 28 cities in outstate Michigan.

1936   Colonel Butterfield dies at age 68 of tuberculosis at the Christian Science Sanitorium in Boston.

1936   Vice President Edward C. Beatty assumes presidency of Butterfield Theatres.

1940s   Butterfield Theatres is operating 96 theatres plus subsidiaries—the largest chain in outstate Michigan.

1980s   Lyle W. Smith is the last Butterfield Theatres president before the theatres are sold to Kerasotes Theatres of Springfield, Illinois.

2002   Joe Sterling, current president of Butterfield Theatres, Inc., oversees the remaining Butterfield properties and assets.

Col. Walter Scott Butterfield
W.S. Butterfield Theatres, Inc.

Col. Walter Scott Butterfield was born in Connersville, Indiana, in 1867. His daughter, Anne Butterfield Handey, described him as a bald, short man standing only 5'6" and weighing 140 pounds. Her 1973 memoir, *A Butterfield Girl Remembers,* also said he was immaculate in appearance and dress.

Colonel Butterfield was married three times. His first wife was the mother of his daughter, Mitties Butterfield Rathbun Mott, who died in 1926. By his second marriage he was the father of four daughters: Mrs. Clarence Allen of Grand Rapids; Mrs. Jesse Page of Charlotte, North Carolina; Ms. Julia Scott Butterfield of Pinehurst, North Carolina; and Mrs. Paul A. Berry of Los Angeles, California. For his third wife he married Irene Daley, the mother of his daughter Anne.

Anne recalled that her father was a "man's man" who enjoyed participating in all sports and attending the big events of the day, such as the Gene Tunney fight and the Kentucky Derby. "Dad was an entrepreneur of the old-school," she said. He became so involved in land that for a while he had his own real estate office at the foot of Gull Lake near Kalamazoo while running the

Butterfield theater chain full time. His wife, Irene, loves to describe the modest sign nailed up beside the doorbell of the little shingled house: "W.S. Butterfield, Real Estate." Under that and even more discreet: "W.S. Butterfield, Christian Science Practitioner." Finally, still lower, a large, hand-lettered sign: "WORMS FOR SALE."

Colonel Butterfield got his start in the theatre business because he didn't want to be a newspaperman. At the age of eighteen he got tired of working at the Columbus, Ohio, newspaper that his father published and went next door to the Grand Theatre, where he became an usher. He worked his way up until, by age twenty-one, he was the theatre's treasurer. At age twenty-three he moved to Chicago, where he worked for a time at the Haymarket Theatre. This first taste of big-time vaudeville soon led to his traveling around the country as manager and booking agent for various troupes.

In 1904 he was beginning to realize his dream of becoming a theatre circuit owner-operator when he built the Henry Boyle Theatre in Fond du Lac, Wisconsin. In 1906, at the advice of Pantages circuit executive Walter Keefe, Butterfield came to Battle Creek, Michigan. He enjoyed the area so much that he decided to stay there.

In Battle Creek, Butterfield leased the Hamblin Opera house for use as a vaudeville theater, renaming it the Bijou in 1906. In 1909, he erected a new Bijou Theatre to replace the old opera house. The new Bijou opened for the first time on September 13, 1909.

In 1911, Butterfield organized Bijou Theatrical Enterprises, Inc., the flagship of which was the Bijou Theater. Within the next five years, he began operating theatres in Jackson, Flint, and Kalamazoo. As the years went by, the

Butterfield empire grew to encompass nearly the entire Lower Peninsula, except for the Detroit area. By March 19, 1928, Butterfield's twenty-second anniversary celebration, he was operating seventy-five theatres in twenty-eight cities.

During this period of expansion, Butterfield moved his corporate office from Battle Creek to Detroit in 1924, changing the name to W.S. Butterfield Theatres, Inc., with a subsidiary company called Butterfield Michigan Theatres, Inc. Also during this time, he acquired the Fitzpatrick & McElroy Michigan Theatres chain, which expanded the company's holdings to Adrian, Alpena, Benton Harbor, Big Rapids, Cadillac, Ludington, Manistee, St. Joseph, Three Rivers, and Traverse City.

His first venture into Grand Rapids came during the summer of 1923, when he leased the Ramona Theatre for a series of summer musicals. In 1926 he purchased Consolidated Theatres Company, which had owned and operated the Majestic Gardens, Orpheum, Isis, and Strand Theatres, and thereby became a permanent part of the area theatre scene. The Orpheum was eventually remodeled and renamed the Kent, while the Strand was ultimately closed and renovated into retail space. A year later, in 1927, when Harry Sommers' lease on the Powers expired, Butterfield also acquired that property.

In 1933, Butterfield strengthened his Grand Rapids holdings by acquiring the Regent and Keith's Theatres from Keith's-Albee Circuit. He brought Walter Norris, who had previously managed the Empress from 1924 to 1930 for Keith's-Albee, back to Grand Rapids to act as his city manager and oversee operations of the Keith's, Regent, and Majestic Theaters. Norris's assistant, Harry Irons, managed the Kent and Isis (Center).

Just prior to his death, he organized a partnership with Allen Johnson to be called Butterfield and Johnson (B & J) Theatres Corporation, with plans already drawn up for what eventually became the Eastown in Grand Rapids. At the time of his death, Butterfield had brought together, by merger with W.S. Butterfield Theaters, Inc., a long list of theatre companies: Bijou Theatrical Company and Consolidated Theaters, of Grand Rapids; the Lansing Arcade and Theater Company; the Flint Regent Theater Company; the Saginaw Franklin Theater Company; the Port Huron Family Theater Company; the Flint Capitol Theater Company; the Ann Arbor Theater Company, and the Gull Lake and Allendale Land companies. At one time there were ninety-six theaters in the chain owned by the company he founded.

In 1928 Butterfield bought out the interests of Glenn A. Cross of Battle Creek, acquiring the Post, Regent, Garden, and Strand Theatres to go along with the Bijou. By the time he died, however, the Garden had been returned to Cross and renamed the Rex.

Colonel Butterfield passed away of tuberculosis at a Christian Science sanatorium in Boston, on April 20, 1936. He was 68. He and his third wife, along with chain vice-president and general manager Edward C. Beatty, had stopped in Boston due to his illness during their return from wintering in Florida. Butterfield was survived by his wife and five of six daughters, also by eight grandchildren, his brother Frank (manager of the Strand in Lansing) and two sisters.

Edward Beatty assumed control of the theatre chain, which, including Butterfield's share of B & J Theatres, then numbered eighty-five theatres in sixteen cities. The Butterfield property on Gull Lake is still one of the finest in

this prestigious lakefront district. Butterfield also had been a director in several Battle Creek industries.

Butterfield never served in the Armed Forces. His title of Colonel was given to him as a nickname by the troops at Camp Custer in Battle Creek as a token of esteem and gratitude for his efforts in keeping morale high by staging vaudeville shows on the base. ∎

Reflections of a Butterfield Theatres Manager

Earl Berry of Flint, Michigan was interviewed by the author in May 2001 about his years as a manager and city manager of the Butterfield movie chain in the Flint area. The following questions and answers reflect his views on the theatre business.

How long were you with Butterfield Theatres?

Earl Berry on the left, with the author.

Berry served 47 years with the Butterfield Theatres between 1937 and 1984. He said he served in the military from 1941 to 1945. His career with Butterfield included doorman, usher, assistant manager, manager, city manager, and regional manager. It was clear that he had worked his way up through the various management positions. He related that he spent most of his years at the Capitol Theatre. Berry met his wife, Vivian Boyce, who was an usher at the Capitol in 1944. They were married and had one daughter, Pamela Berry Peck and a granddaughter.

What was your background to get you into the business?

Berry indicated he graduated from Flint Northern High School, and

then attended Baker Business College. Paul Seippel hired him for a job at the Capitol Theatre.

What were the primary duties of a theatre manager?

Berry indicated that the overall direction of theatre operations, including advertising and promotional materials, was part of his job, in addition to hiring and firing of employees. The theatre manager also reported to Detroit headquarters daily with box office receipts and received any information that the corporate office gave.

What was the most interesting story you remember from your career?

Charlton Heston called to offer a free personal appearance for his first movie, *Dark City*, which Berry was showing. Berry took him up on the offer.

Another time, Pat Boone was making a personal appearance on stage. The stool provided for him had a hole in the middle of the seat, which Boone mentioned to the audience.

During the late 1950s horror film craze, Berry's assistant manager, Bill Kern, would dress up in character and lie in a coffin placed in the lobby of the Garden Theatre. Flint police wanted the coffin removed after receiving complaints from patrons. Once, Kern wandered from theatre to theatre in his costume attracting attention until the police arrested him. Berry had to post his bail the next morning.

What unique problems did you have in the Flint area as city manager?

Berry stated that the Capitol Theatre didn't allow concessions to be sold for a long time, because of the position of importance it had. The management was concerned about the potential messiness the concessions would lead to in the auditorium.

Other than that, Berry said there were few problems, as Flint was considered a good town for seeing movies, and they were a popular form of blue collar entertainment.

Which films made the most impression on you, and why?

Berry mentioned *Gone With the Wind,* which was one of the most popular films ever to play at the Capitol; *Love Story,* which in 1974 set the record as the Capitol's highest grossing film; and also *The Ten Commandments,* which was one of the biggest films to play at the Garden.

He said that the art movies that played at the Garden in its later days were among the things that made a less than favorable impression.

What status did a theatre manager have in the '40s and '50s in the business community?

Berry mentioned that during this time, he was very well known by the upper class and was considered to be an important member of the community. He was on a first-name basis with the mayor and members of the city government.

What was the most rewarding part of the job? The least rewarding?

Berry said that he found the most rewarding part of his job was the pleasure and satisfaction he got from dealing with the public on a daily basis.

The other side of this, the long hours, was one of the least rewarding parts of his job, he added. Theatre managers were expected to work twelve to fourteen hours a day, seven days a week, until 1951, when they were given one day a week off. ∎

William "Emmett" Goodrich
Goodrich Theatres

Born in 1898, William Emmett Goodrich grew up in Grand Rapids. As a youngster he sold papers on downtown street corners, and in his teens and early twenties he worked at American Boxboard. Goodrich enrolled at the University of Michigan, but that was interrupted by a brief stint in the Army during World War I. In his mid-twenties he became a traveling salesman, selling cardboard boxes and other containers. While on the road he began to develop his love for the movie business, rarely missing a chance to attend a movie house wherever he was.

In one of those interesting turns of life, Goodrich's uncle, John Gorman, was a circus clown who went by the name of Shim. Gorman happened to be in the right place at the right time and found himself in a very early movie, *Polly of the Circus.* Through his uncle's contacts, Goodrich found himself talking to a theatre owner in Flint, who told him of a vacant theatre in Grand Rapids. The woman who had been running this theatre as a vaudeville house had been unable to keep up with her rent. This theatre was the Savoy, which, when built in the 1880s, had been called the Columbia and later the Temple.

Goodrich took over the Savoy in 1930, immediately installing a sound system to take advantage of the new "talking pictures." Opening in 1931 with *All's Quiet on the Western Front,* Emmett quickly built up a large clientele who enjoyed the 15-cent price for two features and the chance to see their favorite films again and again. Goodrich's policy was to rebook the most popular

William "Emmett" Goodrich Sr. and Robert Goodrich Jr.

movies and run them as the bottom half of the bill with whatever was the current "must-see" hit.

Goodrich remembers booking *Red River* with John Wayne. "I showed that western film about ten different times," he said. "There were a couple of others I played over and over—Burt Lancaster in *The Crimson Pirate* and Gregory Peck in *The Gunfighter.*" Goodrich was very particular about the films he booked. He went to Detroit every week to screen films and negotiate the rental terms. In the mid-1930s he installed one of Grand Rapids' first air conditioning systems, one that drew its water from a subterranean river flowing from Wisconsin under Lake Michigan.

In 1966 Goodrich retired, turning the Savoy over to his son, Robert (Bob)

Josephine "Josie" Dobrowolski.

Emmett Goodrich. Another son, Tom, also worked for a time at the Savoy. William Emmett Goodrich died on February 10, 1990, at the age of 91, leaving behind his wife, Kathryn, and three children, Robert, Thomas, and Mary Kay.

During the 1970s, all the other downtown Grand Rapids theatres (some seven buildings in all) closed, leaving the Savoy's bright, engaging marquee as a unique city light. Sadly, the Savoy was shut down in 1979 and demolished by the city in 1980 as part of its urban redevelopment.

As the 1960s turned into the 1970s, Bob Goodrich began expansion of the Goodrich Theatre holdings with the Northtown in Grand Rapids. He added drive-in theatres in Manistee, Cadillac, and Big Rapids, bought theatres in Ann Arbor and Cadillac, and built new theatres in Battle Creek and Saginaw. Bob purchased one of the closed downtown Grand Rapids theatres, the Majestic. He reopened and operated it for some five years before selling it to the Blodgett family, who graciously donated it to the Grand Rapids Civic Theatre.

Goodrich Theatres became Goodrich Quality Theatres, Inc. (GQTI), in the 1990s. By year 2000, Bob had added theatres in Illinois, Indiana, Missouri and Kansas, operating 293 screens in thirty-five theatres. ∎

Jack Loeks Theatres

Born in 1918, Jack Loeks became one of the most successful and influential men in the history of the Grand Rapids movie theatre business.

In 1944, Loeks got the idea to open a newsreel theatre in the downtown area after seeing one in New York City. He leased the Powers Theatre and renamed it the Fotonews, where he ran programs showing the newsreels and shorts he thought people would be most interested in. He was right—the Fotonews became one of the more profitable houses in the city.

After World War II, Loeks wanted to change his format and run feature films but was stonewalled by major producers and distributors, as well as the established chains. He would occasionally get a major film that nobody else was willing to run, and because of this he ended up with such films as *The Outlaw,* starring Jane Russell. He showed it during the month of December when the movie business is the slowest and it proved to be a big money maker. *The Outlaw* was bringing in a full house with five-a-day showings. From the high profits and attendance for this film, Loeks quickly gained respectability in the business, but he was still having trouble with the booking system. After an eleven-year battle, he was part of the antitrust suit in 1948 against the studios and distributors, which forced the studios to divest themselves of the theatres they owned.

Loeks called *King Solomon's Mines* and the British film, *Brief Encounter* directed by David Lean, his favorite films. *King Solomon's Mines* made money, but *Brief Encounter* did not. Another high point of Jack's career was getting the opportunity to show *The Sound of Music*. This movie ran for seventy-eight weeks at the Midtown, going through three prints because of its popularity.

Jack Loeks senior and John Loeks Jr. at their corporate office.

Loeks's empire started to grow as he added the Alpine Twin on Alpine and especially the complex on 28th Street that started as the Studio 28 and Little Studio Theatres. He also built the first drive-in theatre in Grand Rapids—the Beltline on 28th Street (now the Studio 28 site). Other drive-ins included the Division, the Plainfield on Plainfield NE, and the Woodland, situated at 28th Street and Broadmore SE. He also purchased three drive-in theatres in Muskegon, including the North, the Arts, and the Getty Drive-In. The Getty is the only drive-in still operating in the Jack Loeks Theatre circuit.

The Studio 28 complex began as a single auditorium, expanding to a twin, then again to become a six-plex. Later Loeks added more screens, as the total rose from six to twelve and then to twenty screens, all under the same roof. The total seating capacity for the twenty screens was almost six thousand people. To make room for this expansion, Loeks closed the Beltline drive-in theatres.

As the empire grew, so did the responsibilities. Jack brought in his son, Jim, and Jim's wife, Barrie, to handle most of the day-to-day operations. In

1990, when Sony Pictures offered Jim and Barrie the chance to run their own chain of theatres, they accepted the offer and left to start Loeks Star Theatres, with theatres in Detroit, Grand Rapids, and Holland.

At age 76 Loeks turned the company over to his son John and retired as CEO in September 1995. John has continued his father's legacy of expansion and innovation with the new Celebration Cinema Theatres, located in Lansing, Mt. Pleasant, and Benton Harbor-St. Joseph. The Jack Loeks Theatre circuit is now completing its most ambitious venture with a new Celebration Cinema and Michigan's only outstate IMAX Theatre in northeast Grand Rapids. This complex opened in 2001. ∎

The Poisson Dynasty

The name Poisson represented a family in Grand Rapids who put a mark on many of the city's second run theatres and other neighborhood movie houses. Through marriage and firsthand experience they were involved in the theatre business for over fifty years.

Joseph H. Poisson

Joseph H. Poisson started out helping his father with the Ramona Park boat operations in the late 1800s. In 1915, at the age of 50, he bought Beecher's Leonard Theatre and renamed it Poisson's. He died at the age of 70, leaving behind four daughters and two sons, Jerome C. and Joseph B. The daughters married Howard T. Reynolds, Oscar Varneau, Roy Muir and Allen Johnson. Each of them—excepting Muir—in turn took control of the Poisson Theatre until they were ready to go out on their own. Joseph B. Poisson worked for Allen Johnson as manager of the Royal in the late 1930s. It is unknown at this time whether Jerome was ever involved in the threatre business.

Howard Reynolds

Howard T. Reynolds married Marie Poisson and eventually owned the Family, Stocking, and Vogue theatres before selling them to Herbert R. Boshoven for $135,000 in 1946. He bought the Michigan Street Theatre in 1938, renaming it the Vogue, and apparently for a time was operating the

Roosevelt theatre with his brother Clifton as manager (1932-1939).

His was a family-run operation, as chronicled by an article in a theatre trade magazine. His wife, Marie, ran the concessions. Two sons, Bob and Dick, each managed a theatre, and a daughter acted as bookkeeper for the chain. Howard died in 1955 at the age of 65, preceded by his brother Clifton in 1951, and apparently also by his son Dick, who may have been killed during World War II. He was survived by Marie, his son Bob, and two daughters.

Oscar Varneau

Oscar Varneau owned and operated the Wealthy Theatre for several years before turning it over to Allen Johnson, who ran it for many years afterwards as a successful art/foreign film house in southeast Grand Rapids.

Allen Johnson

Johnson was probably the most ambitious of the three. Married to Marguerite Poisson, he bought the Royal and Poisson's Leonard theatres from his father-in-law in 1926. He then took a long term lease on Herb Boshoven's Our Theatre beginning in 1930. In 1935-36, he formed a partnership with Col. Water S. Butterfield, creating Butterfield & Johnson Theatres. Edward C. Beatty, Butterfield vice-president and the Colonel's right-hand man, became Johnson's partner after Butterfield's death in April 1936. The partners opened the Eastown in 1936 and the Four-Star in 1938. They later took over control of the Wealthy sometime around 1942. Eventually they fell on hard times, closing Our Theatre in 1946, then losing it back to Boshoven in 1948. The

Allen Johnson

Eastown and Four-Star continued operations until the mid-1960s, at which time Johnson sold his interest in the business sometime between 1962 and 1964.

According to newspaper ads from September 1964, the Four-Star had apparently been sold (sometime after September 1962), since the theatres were running separate features for the first time. Also, the Wealthy was still part of the Eastown operation, but ownership is unclear, as opposed to the 1962 ads which still show them as B & J Theatres.

Johnson died in 1980 at the age of 84, leaving behind a son, Robert Allen Johnson, and a daughter, Louanne Johnson Heidman. ∎

The Evolution of the Movie Palace

A Brief History of the Movie Theatre in the United States

The first theatre devoted exclusively to the showing of motion pictures was the Nickelodeon of Pittsburgh, Pennsylvania, which opened June 19, 1905, in an empty storefront. While this type of theatre was more than adequate for its time, it was plain in appearance and was considered a working-class diversion.

Theatre owners and operators realized that if they were going to succeed in the business, they needed to make the theatres themselves more attractive. In 1914 the era of movie palaces as we know them began with the opening of the Strand in New York City. For the first time, moviegoers could escape the harshness of reality for a few hours by sitting in an elegantly decorated auditorium watching their favorite stars on the silver screen. As public acceptance of the motion picture increased, so did the size and grandeur of the palaces and the reputations of the architects who designed them.

As years went by, theatre designs changed to reflect the fortunes of the American public, until by the late

1940s and early 1950s the emphasis had changed from decorative to functionality. This, unfortunately, meant the end of an era.

The first drive-in theatres appeared on the scene in 1933 on the east coast. They quickly became popular and expanded nationally to over five thousand in 1950. Drive-in theatres allowed parents to bring their children to the movies at bargain prices, with attractions which rivaled a small fair's midway. Prices were usually on a per-car basis, making an evening's entertainment affordable. However, due to a number of factors—including the invention of television, expansion of the suburbs, and the lack of films available to the theatre owners—drive-in theatres began to disappear nationally until there were less than a thousand remaining nationwide in 1990.

The architecture of Michigan drive-in theatres was rather common, and was similar in design and layout according to the property that owners acquired to show films. Michigan drive-ins first appeared in the Detroit area and quickly moved outstate after World War II. The Butterfield chain took advantage of the phenomenon and bought many of the drive-ins in and around the major cities. It is interesting to note that many drive-ins outstate were locally owned during the 1950s. ∎

The Future

As the twenty-first century begins, the movie theatre business in Michigan remains healthy. An expansion of theatre complexes has begun throughout the state. National theatre chains such as AMC and Showcase Cinema still dominate in the Detroit and large metro Michigan areas. Modern theatre chains must have more films in a given area to be profitable. The trend is for a multiplex structure, utilizing a large number of auditoriums under one roof.

A good example of this expansion is the establishment of Neighborhood Cinema Group in 2002. This company owns theatres in Alma, Clio, Coldwater, Greenville, Lansing, Lapeer, Midland, and Owosso. President Gary Geiger says the goal of NCG Theatres is to provide customers with a premier movie-going experience. Geiger sees the future of these cinemas as a niche in smaller communities. The theatres provide small town audiences with a wide range of the current film product in a quiet, comfortable setting with all the amenities of the urban multiplexes: first-run movies, stadium seating, high-back and rocker seats, and the latest sound technology.

Veteran theatre operators in Michigan—Jack Loeks

The new Neighborhood Cinema Group 18-screen multiplex opened November 15, 2002, in Lansing, Michigan.

Gary Geiger, Ed Hilliker and Steve Smith, NCG Cinema

Theatres and Goodrich Quality Theatres, both based in Grand Rapids—have expanded their properties. These chains include large screen complexes, medium size, and smaller types. Loeks also provides Michigan with the only outstate IMAX theatre, located in Grand Rapids. Loeks's IMAX theatre provides the theatre-going audience with a superior projection process utilizing the large screen and Dolby sound.

Bob Goodrich indicates that a new trend in today's theatres is the use of multimedia advertising presentations prior to the showing of the feature film. This is also a new way for theatres to acquire added revenue.

Loeks, Goodrich, and Geiger operate Michigan-based companies with strong roots in the entertainment business, ensuring a winning historical connection, as well as contributing to an expanding Michigan economy for years to come. ∎

Movie Theatre Architecture:
Nationwide and Regional

Several architects dominated the age of the movie palace. Thomas Lamb, a Scot, designed over three hundred theaters. His work was characterized by Italian Renaissance and Neoclassical designs. He was a particular favorite of Marcus Loew of the Loew theater chain.

Lamb's work was flamboyant, while the work of John Eberson was exotic. The Austrian was the originator of the atmospheric "stars and clouds" theaters. Realizing that American audiences desired total fantasy, he created a Spanish patio and an Italian garden at the Capitol Theater in Flint. Eberson's plan for the State in Kalamazoo was known for its rare symmetrical design excepting only the windows and arches.

The first talking picture was presented at an invitational performance on August 5, 1926, at the Warner Theater in New York. Using Vitaphone technology, it featured Mischa Elman, Marion Talley, and Efrem Zimbalist, Sr., among others. The feature film was *Don Juan* starring John Barrymore, Mary

Astor, Warner Oland, Estelle Taylor, and Myrna Loy. The film had no sound recorded on it, but was synchronized with disc phonograph records of the musical score. The first "talkie" was *The Jazz Singer,* which was released the following year.

During the 1930s, theatre design was influenced by the modern style, relying on geometric or organized design patterns. In Detroit, the architect C. Howard Crane built most of the Grand Circus Park theatres, while Rapp and Rapp and John Kunsky designed many others in Detroit, including the Michigan. Often construction was done in Detroit and outstate theatres by local construction companies and suppliers. Theatre owners wanted to use local units to establish and preserve control and to provide good will with local suppliers.

The first theatre to be built in Grand Circus Park was the Madison, which opened on March 7, 1917. It was followed quickly in September of that same year by the Adams. Both of these theatres were built by John Kunsky (1875-1952). Kunsky built many of the major

motion picture theatres in Detroit, including the Capitol (in Grand Circus Park) in 1922 and the State (in Clubland) in 1925. In fact the park became unofficially known as "Kunsky Circle" because of him. The Michigan (1926) was built by the Balaban and Katz Theatre Circuit, but was operated by Kunsky who owned a 72 percent interest in it.

Next was the Oriental (1927), designed in the style the name implies, and the United Artists (1928). The Fox Theatre was built on Woodward at Columbia. It was designed for William Fox by C. Howard Crane, who designed all of the Detroit theatres except the Michigan and Oriental. Its interior combines a blend of Burmese, Hindu, Persian, Indian, and Chinese design elements. This style has been nicknamed "Siamese Byzantine."

Motion picture theatres flourished in Detroit during the 1930s and 40s, but after World War II attendance declined due to the advent of television and the growth of the suburbs. In the 1950s the Oriental's auditorium was demolished for a parking lot and the other theatres fell into disrepair. In 1975 the interior furnishings of the United Artists were auctioned off and the auditorium was used sporadically by the Detroit Symphony Orchestra for recordings. In 1977 the

Michigan was gutted and turned into a three-level parking garage. Most of the remaining theatres stopped showing films and eventually closed.

Currently, Grand Circus Park is being revitalized into Detroit's entertainment district once again. Several theatres and restaurants have opened, and restoration and building projects are currently in progress.

Outstate, architects noted for theatre design in Michigan include Rapp and Rapp, and Maurice Finkel in Detroit, Jackson, Grand Rapids and Ann Arbor. Osgood and Osgood contributed to Saginaw's Temple Theatre construction. In Grand Rapids, the Ebel Construction company built the Eastown and Four Star theatres, both of which were owned by Allen Johnson of B & J Theatres. Johnson used the Grand Rapids-based American Seating Company for interior seats in his theatres, as did many other owners throughout the state. As well as designing the above mentioned Detroit theatres, C. Howard Crane also designed the Bay State in Bay City.

Dutch and Nordic style architecture dominated Upper Peninsula theatre design. Michael Hare, architect, and James Miller, contractor, worked on several theatres in Marquette, Escanaba, and Ishpeming. ∎

Keith's Theatre, Grand Rapids, Michigan

Keith's Theatre, Grand Rapids, Michigan

Michigan Theatre, Jackson, Michigan

Keith's Theatre, Grand Rapids, Michigan

Majestic Theatre, Grand Rapids, Michigan

Strand/Michigan Theatre—then and today, Lansing, Michigan

Movie Theatre Advertising

Promotion of movies in Michigan theatres was done in the 1930s through 1950s in three major ways: newspapers, posters, and electronic media. These were the general sources of information that most of the community used to find out about films in their area. First run theatres had the largest, most appealing ads, often subsidized by the movie distributors. The most interesting ads would usually appear the day before the film opened, or in the Sunday editions of the newspaper. Sub run theatres often had no more than just a mention of the film title and the times it was to be shown. The theatre's newspaper advertising budget was usually the largest item that theatre owners had to be concerned about. Advertising slicks and press books were sent to theatres prior to the movie's release, so that the manager could make up the individual ads for the run. This was usually done on a weekly basis. Butterfield Theatres had the city manager in the larger cities responsible for placing the ads in their city. Deadlines were often determined by the newspaper itself. Special feature stories about first run films and stars were often printed in local newspapers as part of the entertainment section.

Film booking was done in Detroit at the various film exchanges. Most first run theatres had their own bookers, but occasionally, a single theatre owner would book all his own product. Films were screened weekly, making it necessary to make a trip to Detroit by the theatre owners. Jack Loeks, of Grand Rapids, often flew his own plane to Detroit for booking trips. Colonel Butterfield, in the 1920s, would ride the train from Battle Creek to Detroit to oversee operations.

National Screen Service handled all the other related promotional material for the films, including posters and trailers. Until the 1980s, National Screen Service materials had to be returned to Detroit for reuse by other theatres in the state. Posters were often sent directly to the theatre with the print of the film. By the time sub run theatres received these materials, many of the posters showed wear and tear.

Electronic media exploitation consisted of radio, and later, television, advertising. Some of the advertising was little more than audio and video trailers of the feature film shown in the local theatres. Major radio and television programs often would interview stars of an upcoming movie release that was playing in the first run theatres. This practice has not changed much in today's current Michigan theatre advertising campaigns. ∎

Typical advertising circa 1916, Lansing, Michigan

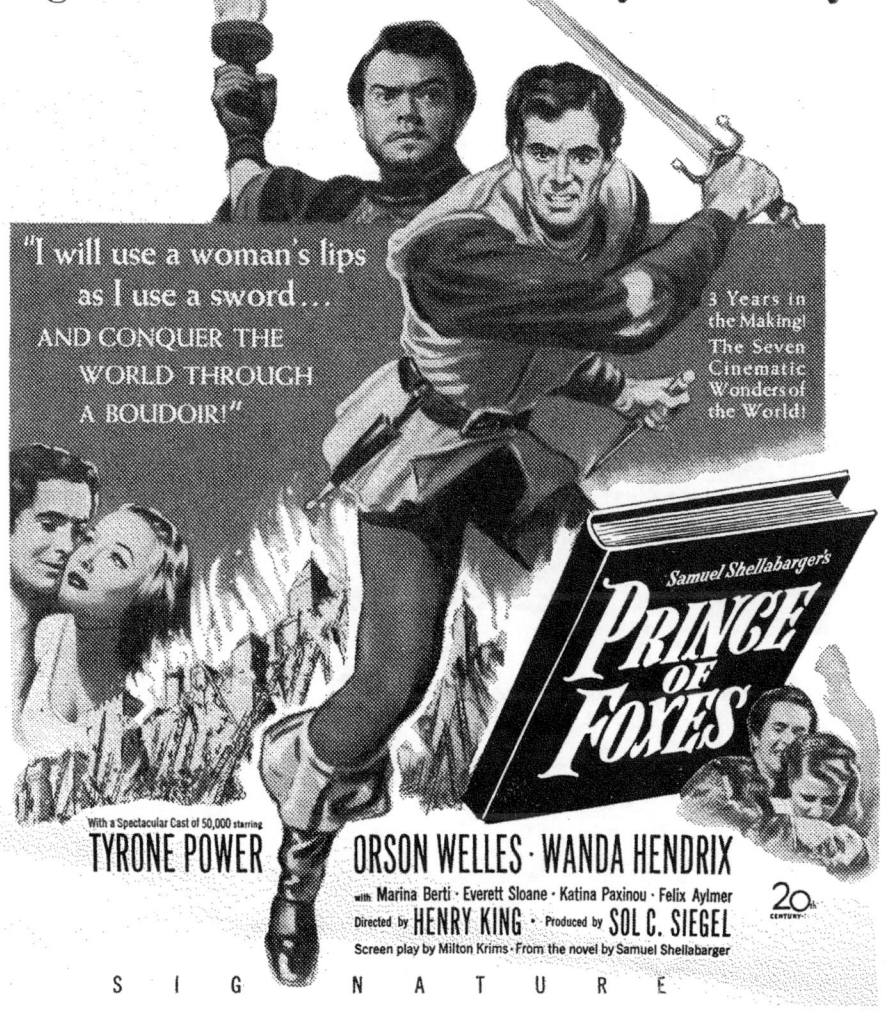

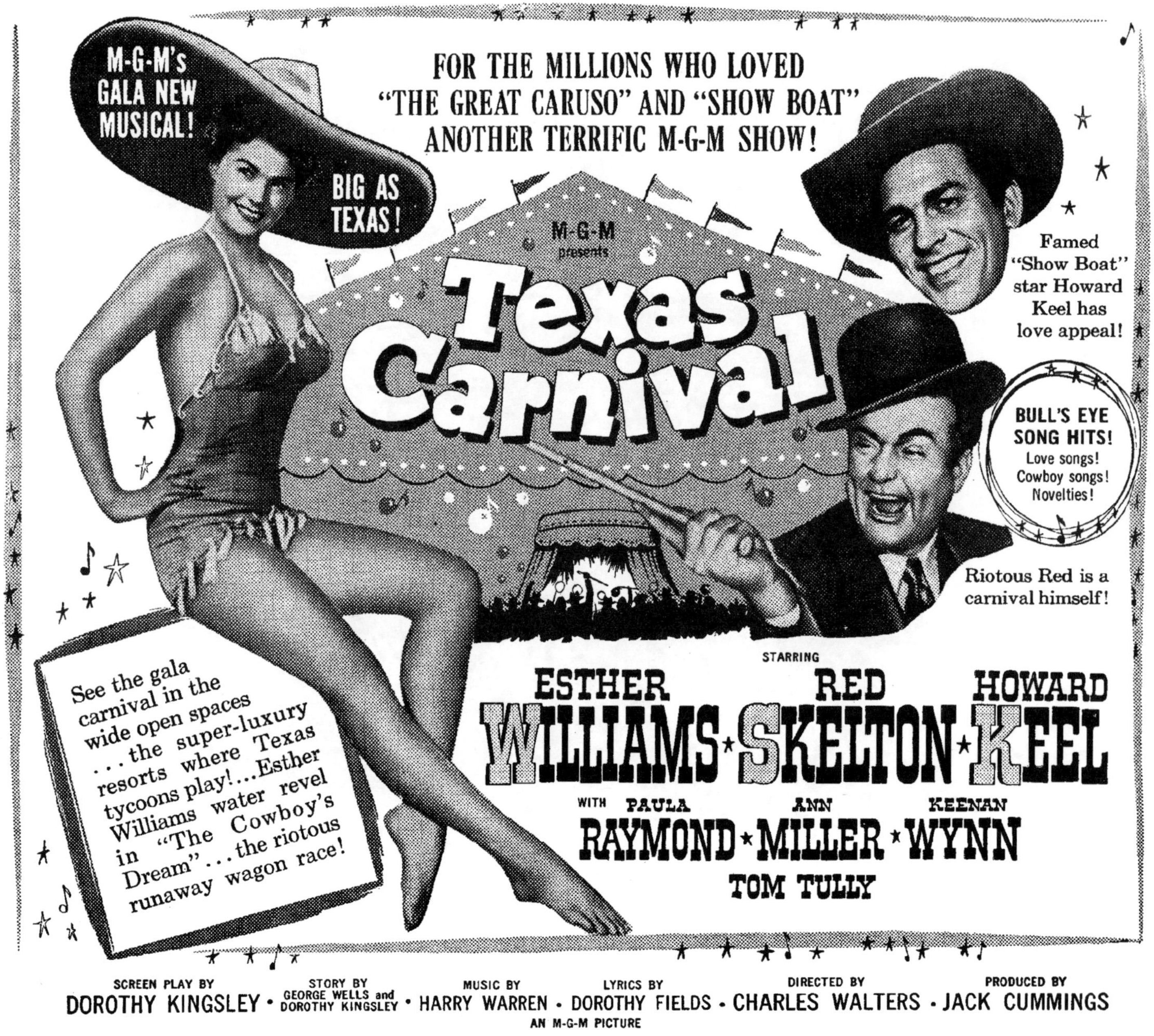
M-G-M's GALA NEW MUSICAL!
BIG AS TEXAS!
FOR THE MILLIONS WHO LOVED "THE GREAT CARUSO" AND "SHOW BOAT" ANOTHER TERRIFIC M-G-M SHOW!
M-G-M presents
Texas Carnival
Famed "Show Boat" star Howard Keel has love appeal!
BULL'S EYE SONG HITS! Love songs! Cowboy songs! Novelties!
Riotous Red is a carnival himself!
See the gala carnival in the wide open spaces . . . the super-luxury resorts where Texas tycoons play! ... Esther Williams water revel in "The Cowboy's Dream" ... the riotous runaway wagon race!
STARRING
ESTHER WILLIAMS ★ RED SKELTON ★ HOWARD KEEL
WITH PAULA RAYMOND ★ ANN MILLER ★ KEENAN WYNN
TOM TULLY
SCREEN PLAY BY DOROTHY KINGSLEY • STORY BY GEORGE WELLS and DOROTHY KINGSLEY • MUSIC BY HARRY WARREN • LYRICS BY DOROTHY FIELDS • DIRECTED BY CHARLES WALTERS • PRODUCED BY JACK CUMMINGS
AN M-G-M PICTURE

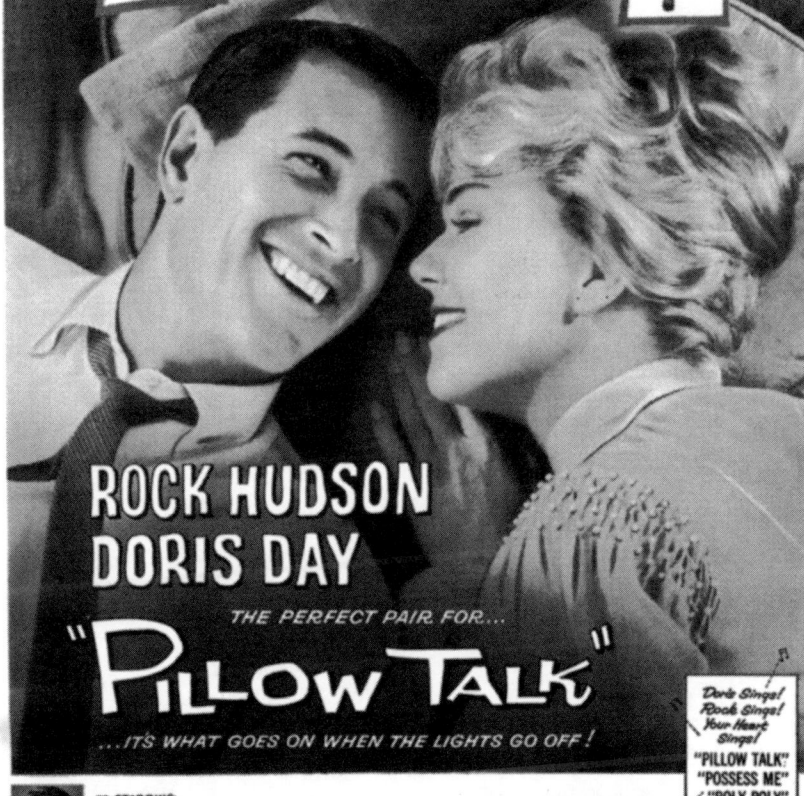

Lower Peninsula Theatres
Theatre Gallery

Ann Arbor

The Michigan Theatre was known as the flagship for the W. S. Butterfield chain in Ann Arbor. It has a Romanesque revival exterior. The balcony was semi-circular and had a split grand staircase. The original bronze drinking fountains were restored in the 1980s and the original Wurlitzer pipe organ was reinstalled. The lobby of the Michigan features a grand staircase, mirrored walls and a gilded ceiling. The theatre still provides the community with special film showings and stage presentations, supported by donations and the sale of annual memberships.

Ann Arbor

Michigan Theatre

City:
Ann Arbor, Michigan

Address:
603 E. Liberty

Owner:
Butterfield Theatres

Built:
1928

Seating:
1,800

Film Release:
First Run

Present Status:
Movies, concerts, special events

Ann Arbor

State Theatre

City:
Ann Arbor, Michigan

Address:
233 S. State Street

Owner:
Butterfield Theatres

Built:
1945

Seating:
950

Film Release:
First Run

Present Status:
Concerts, special events

Ann Arbor

Campus Theatre

City:
Ann Arbor, Michigan

Address:
1214 S. University

Owner:
Butterfield Theatres

Built:
1956

Seating:
900

Film Release:
First Run

Present Status:
Closed

Battle Creek

Battle Creek was the flagship city for the Butterfield Theatres. Colonel Butterfield resided in Battle Creek, even though he moved his corporate office to Detroit to be closer to the film distributors. The Bijou became his main theatre and was located on West Michigan Avenue, on the site of the former Hamblin Opera House, which had been destroyed in a fire and razed.

Butterfield soon acquired other theatres in Battle Creek, but maintained the Bijou as his primary first-run house.

A unique architectural feature of the Bijou was the arcade, which included other businesses. The arcade was a source of additional income for the theatre. The façade of the Bijou was quite ordinary and by no means represented the best of the Butterfield Theatres in Michigan.

Battle Creek

Hamblin Opera House

City:
Battle Creek, Michigan

Address:
45 West Michigan

Owner:
Butterfield Theatres

Built:
1869

Seating:
400

Film Release:
Silents, vaudeville

Present Status:
Demolished after a fire

Battle Creek

Bijou Theatre

City:
Battle Creek, Michigan

Address:
45 West Michigan

Owner:
Butterfield Theatres

Built:
1909
(replacing the Hamblin Opera House)

Seating:
1,053

Film Release:
First Run

Present Status:
Riverwalk Center Parking Lot

Bay City

The State Theatre is one of the only four Mayan temple style theatres remaining in the United States. Originally the theatre was part of the Butterfield chain and showed first run movies only. Its 1950s V-shaped neon marquee remains intact. C. Howard Crane was response for the State's original design. Today the Friends of the State Theatre have embarked on an extensive renovation campaign. The theatre designers plan to use remaining original architectural drawings and pictures to reconstruct destroyed areas of the building. Their focus is to create a cultural and entertainment center for the entire community.

Bay City

State Theatre
(Bay, Orpheum)

City:
Bay City, Michigan

Address:
913 Washington

Owner:
Butterfield Theatres

Built:
1927

Seating:
778

Film Release:
First Run

Present Status:
Bay City Performing Arts Center

Bay City

Empire Theatre

City:
Bay City, Michigan

Address:
Washington Avenue

Owner:
Narlock Enterprises

Built:
1947

Seating:
1,200

Film Release:
First Run

Present Status:
Nightclub

Bay City

Colonial Theatre
(Bay City)

City:
Bay City, Michigan

Address:
1405 Woodside Ave., Essexville

Owner:
Thomas Arnold, Al Hamlin, Louis Kempa

Built:
1948

Seating:
500

Film Release:
Sub Run

Present Status:
Closed, for lease

Detroit

Grand Circus Park, once a residential district, became Detroit's "theatre row" shortly after the turn of the century. Most of the first-run theatres were built then, and all of them faced Grand Circus Park or one of its spokes. The majority of the Detroit theatres were part of John Kunsky's holdings. Kunsky was a theatre magnate at that time.

C. Howard Crane designed most of the Grand Circus Park theatres. Most of the theatres of the area are known for their anonymous entrances. These theatres were part of office complexes in the block. Ornamental schemes included window placement, which helped differentiate one theatre from another. Marquees, verticals, and roof signs were also part of the Grand Circus Park theatres. Spanish Gothic was used for the design of the United Artists Theatre. The Michigan was Detroit's second-largest theatre, with the only architecturally designed entrance. The Michigan's vertical sign was replaced in 1960 with square, changeable light bulbs bordered by neon. The marquee was changed to the more common lighted background, illuminating letters that spelled out the film's title.

Detroit

Fox Theatre

City:
Detroit, Michigan

Address:
Woodward at Columbia

Owner:
Ilitch Enterprises

Built:
1928

Seating:
5,041

Film Release:
First Run

Present Status:
Still in operation

Detroit

State Theatre
(Palms)

City:
Detroit, Michigan

Address:
2111 Woodward

Owner:
Kunsky, Balaban & Katz, Publix Theatres

Built:
1925, renamed 1937

Seating:
2,967

Film Release:
First Run

Present Status:
Clubland dance club

Detroit

Madison Theatre

City:
Detroit, Michigan

Address:
22 Witherall

Owner:
Kunsky, Balaban & Katz, Publix Theatres

Built:
1917

Seating:
1,806

Film Release:
First Run

Present Status:
Michigan Opera Theatre, small theatrical productions

Detroit

Gem Theatre
(Cinema)

City:
Detroit, Michigan

Address:
33 Madison

Owner:
Kunsky, Balaban & Katz, Publix Theatres

Built:
1928

Seating:
457

Film Release:
Art/Foreign Films

Present Status:
Supper club/dinner theatre

Detroit

Capitol Theatre
(Grand Circus)

City:
Detroit, Michigan

Address:
1526 Broadway

Owner:
Kunsky, Balaban & Katz, Publix Theatres

Built:
1922, renamed 1960

Seating:
4,250

Film Release:
First Run

Present Status:
Detroit Grand Opera House

Detroit

Wilson Theatre
(Cinerama, Music Hall)

City:
Detroit, Michigan

Address:
350 Madison

Owner:
Matilda Dodge Wilson, Cinerama Corporation

Built:
1928

Seating:
1,880

Film Release:
First Run/Cinerama

Present Status:
Live theatre

Detroit

United Artists Theatre

City:
Detroit, Michigan

Address:
140 Bagley

Owner:
United Artists Corporation

Built:
1928

Seating:
2,070

Film Release:
First Run

Present Status:
Night club, office and apartment building

Detroit

Michigan Theatre

City:
Detroit, Michigan

Address:
Bagley at Clifford

Owner:
Kunsky, Balaban & Katz, Publix Theatres

Built:
1926

Seating:
4,038

Film Release:
First Run

Present Status:
Parking garage

Detroit

Adams Theatre

City:
Detroit, Michigan

Address:
44 W. Adams

Owner:
Kunsky, Balaban & Katz, Publix Theatres

Built:
1917

Seating:
1,770

Film Release:
First Run

Present Status:
Theatre closed 1988

Detroit

Redford Theatre

City:
Detroit, Michigan

Address:
17354 Lahser Road at Grand River

Owner:
John Kunsky, Motor City Theatre Organ Society

Built:
1928

Seating:
2,000 originally, 1,600 today

Film Release:
First Run

Present Status:
Restored. Today it features classic films and organ recitals.

Detroit

Harper Theatre

City:
Detroit, Michigan

Address:
14238 Harper Ave. & Lakewood St.

Owner:
Whisper & Wetsman Theatres

Built:
1939

Seating:
1,975

Film Release:
First Run

Present Status:
Harpo's Night Club

Detroit

Hollywood Theatre

City:
Detroit, Michigan

Address:
4801 W. Fort St. at Ferdinand St.

Owner:
Ben & Lou Cohen

Built:
1927

Seating:
3,436

Film Release:
First Run

Present Status:
Parking Lot

Detroit

Duke Theatre

City:
Detroit, Michigan

Address:
W. 8 Mile Road at Wyoming

Owner:
Whisper & Wetsman Theatres,
Saul Korman

Built:
1947

Seating:
1,500

Film Release:
Second Run

Present Status:
Closed 1953

Flint

The Capitol Theatre in Flint was another design masterpiece of John Eberson. The exterior decoration of the theatre and its surroundings included a full block which included office rental space. The original opening publicity of the Capitol Theatre mentioned its interesting fifteenth-century Hispano-Italian style. Extensive renovation was done in 1957 and many ornate statues and artworks were eliminated from the building. The Barton organ was donated to the Flint Institute of Arts. The vertical sign displaying the letters "CAPITOL" on the marquee were made of terra cotta and are still visible to the public.

Flint

Capitol Theatre

City:
Flint, Michigan

Address:
140-142 E. Second Street

Owner:
Butterfield Theatres

Built:
1927

Seating:
1,900

Film Release:
First Run

Present Status:
Closed 1984, building still standing

Flint

Regent Theatre

City:
Flint, Michigan

Address:
906 N. Saginaw

Owner:
Butterfield Theatres

Built:
1918

Seating:
1,600

Film Release:
First Run

Present Status:
Windmill Place restaurant

Flint

Palace Theatre

City:
Flint, Michigan

Address:
205 E. Kearsley

Owner:
Butterfield Theatres

Built:
1917

Seating:
1,430

Film Release:
First Run

Present Status:
University of Michigan-Flint Theatre

Flint

Rialto Theatre
(Savoy, New Savoy, Royal)

City:
Flint, Michigan

Address:
308 S. Saginaw

Owner:
Louis Sunlin, Abraham Eiseman

Built:
1908

Seating:
650

Film Release:
Second run, double feature, open 24 hours

Present Status:
Citizens Bank Building

Flint

Della Theatre

City:
Flint, Michigan

Address:
807 Welch Blvd.

Owner:
Matt Theatres

Built:
1937

Seating:
1,200

Film Release:
Second Run

Present Status:
Enterprise Community Investment Company parking lot

Flint

Michigan Theatre

City:
Flint, Michigan

Address:
1614 S. Saginaw

Owner:
Abraham Eiseman, Butterfield Theatres

Built:
1929

Seating:
1,500

Film Release:
Second Run

Present Status:
Julie's Pawn Shop and parking lot

Flint

Garden Theatre

City:
Flint, Michigan

Address:
124 E. First Street

Owner:
Butterfield Theatres

Built:
1939

Seating:
950

Film Release:
First Run

Present Status:
Parking lot opposite Genesee Towers building

Grand Rapids

The Regent was the largest and most elegant of the Grand Rapids theatres. It was built at a cost of about $1 million in 1923. The theatre featured a marble floor lobby with ornate decorations and an auditorium with an arch over the stage area. The area above the auditorium was once a ballroom and later a bowling alley. The Regent also showcased first-rate touring companies that featured vaudeville and Broadway's finest plays.

The Keith's was the other downtown theatre. It was similar to the Regent and was known for its vaudeville presentations from the Keith-Albee circuit. At one time, both theatres were part of the RKO theatre chain.

A comprehensive listing is included for the reader to discover the vastness and importance of Grand Rapids theatres from the 1920s to the present.

Grand Rapids Neighborhood Theatre Directory

(*Denotes theatre still in operation)

Theatre	Other Names	Ownership	Address
Eastown		B&J Theatres	1470 Lake Drive SE
Our		Boshoven/Busic	737 Leonard NW
4-Star		B&J Theatres	1950 Division S
Wealthy		Allen Johnson	1130 Wealthy SE
Royal		Allen Johnson	306 Leonard NW
Liberty	Beecher's Liberty	Willer-Boshoven Theatres	1028 Division S.
Madison		Boshoven/Busic	1231 Madison SE
Franklin	(Beecher's Division)	Willer/Boshoven	814 Division S
Family	(Cinema)	Boshoven/Busic	345 Michigan NE
Capri	(Burton)	Willer/Boshoven	2028 Division S.
State		Willer/Boshoven	543 Stocking Ave. NW
Biltmore	(Beecher's Biltmore)	Willer/Boshoven	963 Cherry SE
Stocking	(Brown's Stocking Av.)	Herb Boshoven Jr.	634 Stocking Ave. NW at Fourth
Vogue	(Michigan Street)	Herb Boshoven Jr.	710 Michigan NE
Fairmount	(Roxy)	Herb Boshoven Jr.	2150 Plainfield NE
Uptown	(Rivoli, Nichols)	Frank Kleaver	404 Division S.
Town	(Alcazar, Roosevelt)	Willer/Boshoven	642 Bridge NW
Southlawn		Grand Rapids Amusement Co.	4002 Division S.
Park		L. & M. Struik	433 Park NE
Galewood		Nathan McCarty	1051 Burton SW
Ramona	(Ramona Gardens)	Goodrich	Wealthy at Lakeside SE, East Grand Rapids
Creston		S. Harry Himelstein	1516 Plainfield NE
Crestonette Vaudette		G. Glenn Fleser	1408 Plainfield NE
Grand		Howard Sturgis	3574 Chicago Dr. SW
Fulton		Leo G. Robinson	806 Fulton SE
Poisson's	(Leonard; Beecher's)	Joseph H. Poisson	419 Leonard NW
Beecher's Surprise	(Surprise)	Beecher's Inc.	303 Michigan NE
Northtown		Robert Goodrich	3494 Plainfield NE
Alpine Twin		Jack Loeks Theatres	Alpine SW
Eastbrook		Kerasotes (Butterfield)	Eastbrook Mall (28th St., now Club Eastbrook nightclub
Studio 28*		Jack Loeks Theatres	28th St.
Little Studio		Jack Loeks Theatres	28th St. (became part of Studio 28)
Movies at Woodland		United Artists Theatres	Woodland Mall (28th St. SE)
Movies at North Kent		United Artists Theatres	North Kent Mall (Plainfield NE)
Showcase Cinemas*		Redstone Theatres	28th St. SE at I-96
Star*		Star Theatres	Alpine NW at I-96
Cinemark*			Grandville Mall
Celebration Cinemas/IMAX Theatre*		Jack Loeks Theatres	Knapp at East Beltline NE (opened 2001)

Grand Rapids

Regent Theatre

City:
Grand Rapids, Michigan

Address:
133 Crescent

Owner:
RKO, Butterfield Theatres

Built:
1923

Seating:
2,000

Film Release:
First Run

Present Status:
Closed 1964, demolished in 1978 as part of downtown development

Grand Rapids

Keith's Theatre
(RKO, Empress)

City:
Grand Rapids, Michigan

Address:
113-121 Lyon

Owner:
B.F. Keith, Empress Theatre Co., RKO, Butterfield Theatres

Built:
1914

Seating:
1,900

Film Release:
First Run

Present Status:
Demolished as part of downtown redevelopment

Grand Rapids

Majestic Theatre
(Majestic Gardens)

City:
Grand Rapids, Michigan

Address:
34 Division

Owner:
Consolidated Theatres, Butterfield Theatres, Goodrich Theatres

Built:
1903

Seating:
1,200

Film Release:
First Run

Present Status:
Remodeled, operated by Grand Rapids Civic Theatre

Grand Rapids

Midtown Theatre
(Fotonews, Powers)

City:
Grand Rapids, Michigan

Address:
123 Pearl

Owner:
Jack Loeks Theatres

Built:
1880s, remodeled as Midtown in 1948

Seating:
1,200

Film Release:
First Run

Present Status:
Demolished 1978 as part of downtown redevelopment

Grand Rapids

Center Theatre
(Isis)

City:
Grand Rapids, Michigan

Address:
240-242 Monroe

Owner:
Butterfield Theatres

Built:
1915

Seating:
937

Film Release:
Second Run

Present Status:
Demolished as part of downtown redevelopment

Grand Rapids

Kent Theatre
(Orpheum)

City:
Grand Rapids, Michigan

Address:
322 Monroe

Owner:
Butterfield Theatres

Built:
1930

Seating:
1,000

Film Release:
First Run

Present Status:
Demolished as part of downtown redevelopment

Grand Rapids

Savoy Theatre
(Temple, Columbia)

City:
Grand Rapids, Michigan

Address:
80 Market

Owner:
Goodrich Theatres

Built:
1880s

Seating:
1,000

Film Release:
Second Run

Present Status:
Demolished as part of downtown redevelopment

Grand Rapids

Eastown Theatre

City:
Grand Rapids, Michigan

Address:
1470 Lake Drive SE

Owner:
B&J Theatres

Built:
1936

Seating:
1,000

Film Release:
Second Run

Present Status:
Renovated in the 1990s for use by Temple Evangelical Church

Grand Rapids

Our Theatre

City:
Grand Rapids, Michigan

Address:
737 Leonard NW

Owner:
Willer-Boshoven Theatres,
B&J Theatres,
Boshoven-Busic Theatres

Built:
1928

Seating:
700

Film Release:
Second Run

Present Status:
Closed, building for sale.

Grand Rapids

Four Star Theatre

City:
Grand Rapids, Michigan

Address:
1950 Division S.

Owner:
B&J Theatres

Built:
1938

Seating:
925

Film Release:
Second Run

Present Status:
Closed, occupied by neighborhood youth club, façade remains.

Grand Rapids

Wealthy Theatre

City:
Grand Rapids, Michigan

Address:
1130 Wealthy

Owner:
Allen Johnson (Oscar Varneau)

Built:
1911

Seating:
578

Film Release:
Foreign Films

Present Status:
Renovated 1990s as Wealthy Theatre—neighborhood stage theatre and museum

Jackson

The Michigan Theatre, a Maurice Finkel design, has been partially refurbished and is back in operation in downtown Jackson. The Michigan has an interior treatment of both Renaissance and Art Deco. The lower walls of the auditorium are Baroque and Renaissance in composition. The narrow entry façade is pure Deco with a Moorish, Spanish Colonial terra cotta tower. The Michigan's marquee has been totally restored and provides a home for special theatre presentations. The Barton organ is also being utilized again for special concerts.

Jackson

Michigan Theatre

City:
Jackson, Michigan

Address:
124 N. Mechanic

Owner:
Butterfield Theatres

Built:
1930

Seating:
1,739

Film Release:
First Run

Present Status:
Operated by the
Theatre Preservation Association

Jackson

Regent Theatre

City:
Jackson, Michigan

Address:
172 W. Michigan

Owner:
Butterfield Theatres

Built:
1900s

Seating:
1,600

Film Release:
First Run

Present Status:
Closed, parking lot

Kalamazoo

The State was the primary theatre in Kalamazoo and was designed by John Eberson. The theatre had an atmospheric style and the auditorium was illuminated as a Spanish courtyard, with Renaissance statues placed near the spans of the balcony. A Moorish flavor dominates the interior of the building. The lobby tile favored a Spanish patio. Although the theatre is no longer used as a movie house, the asbestos curtain and the original Barton organ remain intact, and it frequently hosts concerts and special productions.

Kalamazoo

State Theatre

City:
Kalamazoo, Michigan

Address:
404 S. Burdick

Owner:
Butterfield Theatres

Built:
1927

Seating:
1,800

Film Release:
First Run

Present Status:
Stage shows, special events

Kalamazoo

Michigan Theatre

City:
Kalamazoo, Michigan

Address:
12 E. Michigan

Owner:
Butterfield Theatres

Built:
1900s

Seating:
600

Film Release:
First Run

Present Status:
Closed

Kalamazoo

Fuller Theatre

City:
Kalamazoo, Michigan

Address:
225 S. Burdick

Owner:
Butterfield Theatres

Built:
1900s

Seating:
1,500

Film Release:
First Run

Present Status:
Parking lot, Angels & Things Gallery and Gifts

Kalamazoo

Uptown Theatre

City:
Kalamazoo, Michigan

Address:
N. Burdick at Eleanor

Owner:
Kalamazoo Theatre Corp.,
Butterfield Theatres

Built:
1938

Seating:
750

Film Release:
First Run

Present Status:
Demolished

Lansing

Although Lansing's Michigan and Gladmer Theatres were the premier first run houses for most of their history, they were located in the downtown area and did not provide access for students who were attending Michigan State University during an era when student automobiles were a luxury. The Lucon, later to become the Campus, in East Lansing was to become the most modern and important theatre of the Butterfield houses in greater Lansing. A chronological view of this theatre gives the reader a detailed history of one movie house before it was torn down.

Lansing

Strand Theatre
(Michigan)

City:
Lansing, Michigan

Address:
122 S. Washington Avenue

Owner:
Butterfield Theatres

Built:
1921

Seating:
2,000

Film Release:
First Run

Present Status:
Atrium only remains as an office building

Lansing

Gladmer Theatre

City:
Lansing, Michigan

Address:
N. Washington Avenue

Owner:
Butterfield Theatres

Built:
Remodeled 1939 after a fire

Seating:
1,060

Film Release:
First Run

Present Status:
Ameritech parking lot

Lansing

Capitol Theatre

City:
Lansing, Michigan

Address:
204 N. Washington

Owner:
Claude Cady, Butterfield Theatres

Built:
1910

Seating:
750

Film Release:
First Run

Present Status:
Office building

Lansing

Lansing Theatre
(Colonial, Esquire)

City:
Lansing, Michigan

Address:
122 E. Michigan

Owner:
Claude Cady, Butterfield Theatres

Built:
1900

Seating:
750

Film Release:
First Run

Present Status:
Parking lot

Lansing

Orpheum Theatre

City:
Lansing, Michigan

Address:
114 N. Washington

Owner:
Clement Jarvis

Built:
1910

Seating:
400

Film Release:
Second Run

Present Status:
Office building

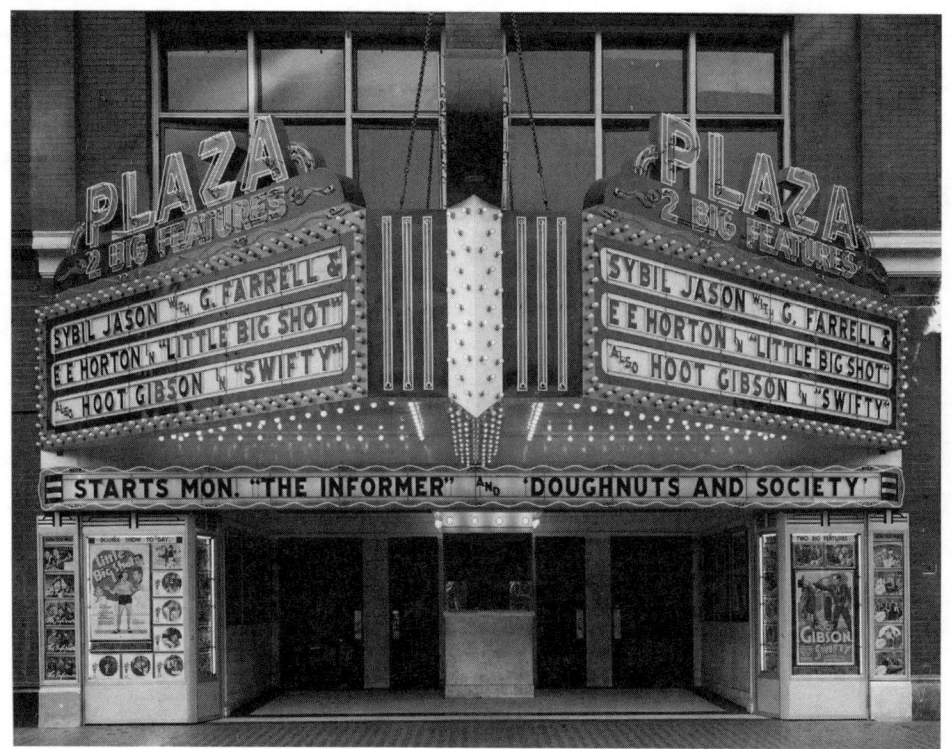

Lansing

Plaza Theatre

City:
Lansing, Michigan

Address:
211 N. Washington

Owner:
Butterfield Theatres

Built:
1914

Seating:
600

Film Release:
Second Run

Present Status:
Office building

Lansing

Northtown Theatre

City:
Lansing, Michigan

Address:
E. Grand River

Owner:
Butterfield Theatres

Built:
Early 1920s

Seating:
600

Film Release:
Second Run

Present Status:
Parking lot, vacant lot

East Lansing

Lucon Theatre
(Campus)

City:
East Lansing, Michigan

Address:
407 E. Grand River

Owner:
Cohen Brothers. Butterfield Theatres, Kerasotes Theatres

Built:
1950

Seating:
1,500

Film Release:
First Run

Present Status:
Renovated 1987-88 as addition to MSU Student Bookstore

East Lansing

The Lucon Theatre opened December 10, 1950, at 407 E. Grand River. The theatre was in the Lucon Building. The Lucon was owned by the Cohen brothers of Detroit. The first manager was Louis Rosenfeld.

The first film shown at the Lucon was *The Glass Menagerie* starring Jane Wyman. The theatre was a first run venue and often showed double features.

The Lucon was an Art Deco design of the 1950s and had 1,500 seats. A crying room with the latest theatre decor of the times was provided for children.

The Lucon eventually was sold to the Butterfield Theatre chain, which owned most first run theatres in outstate Michigan. Rosenfeld was retained as manager, and the name was changed to the Campus.

The Campus opened July 13, 1962, showing *The Notorious Landlady* starring Kim Novak and Jack Lemmon. Some renovating was done to the Campus, notably new seats and changes to the lobby. The theatre continued to show first run movies.

Butterfield Theatre twinned the Campus on September 5, 1980, and showed two first run films. Each auditorium had 525 seats.

Kerasotes Theatres of Springfield, Illinois, purchased the Campus in 1985 and made a number of cost saving decisions, including firing union projectionists.

In June 1987 the Campus was closed, showing *Beverly Hills Cop II* and *Blood Diner* as its last picture shows. Attendance was dismal.

The Campus was purchased by the Student Book Store, which tried to rent it as a theatre but to no avail. The Student Book Store had the theatre destroyed and expanded its business to include the 407 E. Grand River address.

The Campus Theatre marquee sign remains in private hands as the only historic memory of this East Lansing theatre.

East Lansing

State Theatre

City:
East Lansing, Michigan

Address:
215 Abbott Road

Owner:
Butterfield Theatres

Built:
1927

Seating:
800

Film Release:
First Run

Present Status:
Parking lot

Pontiac

The Strand was built to provide entertainment for throngs of auto workers drawn to Pontiac by General Motors. The theatre was originally designed by local architect Leo J. Heenan and was a three-story Renaissance style brick and stone building. Its beauty represented the eighteenth-century English theatre design. The theatre was originally a movie house but has been restructured by a local cultural group to become the hub of the Pontiac theatre district. Ethnic films, festivals, and corporate functions are some of the special events that will take place in the newly renovated Strand Theatre district.

Pontiac

Strand Theatre
(Campus)

City:
Pontiac, Michigan

Address:
1016 N. Saginaw St.

Owner:
Butterfield Theatres

Built:
1921

Seating:
1,175

Film Release:
First Run

Present Status:
Renovated by Strand Theatre Center Inc. Used for movies, stage presentations and community concerts

Saginaw

The Temple Theatre was built in Saginaw in a record six weeks. The theatre was known for its elaborate vaudeville programs and hosted the top acts of the 1920s and 1930s. Butterfield Theatres, Inc., made the Temple Theatre their flagship house in Saginaw. Some of the original theatre stage equipment was preserved and is still used on a limited basis.

Saginaw

Temple Theatre

City:
Saginaw, Michigan

Address:
203 N. Washington

Owner:
Butterfield Theatres

Built:
1917

Seating:
2,239

Film Release:
First Run

Present Status:
Stage shows, selected concerts and special events

Saginaw

Franklin Theatre

City:
Saginaw, Michigan

Address:
132 S. Franklin

Owner:
Butterfield Theatres

Built:
1920

Seating:
1,425

Film Release:
First Run

Present Status:
Parking lot

Upper Peninsula Theatres
Theatre Gallery

Upper Peninsula

The Delft and the Nordic in Marquette were probably the most interesting of the Upper Peninsula theatres, both in architecture and entertainment. Huge murals adorned the Delft auditorium, representing hillsides dotted with trees and covered with snow. Cotton clouds drifted over a blue sky. When renovation occurred in the 1980s, the landscape murals disappeared. A new concession stand, airline lighting along the aisles, and new restrooms were part of the changes. The Delft Theatre had an interesting marquee on Washington Street, but the patrons had to walk around the corner to Main Street to buy their tickets.

Escanaba

Michigan Theatre

City:
Escanaba, Michigan

Address:
811 Ludington

Owner:
Edward Butler

Built:
1915

Seating:
600

Film Release:
First Run

Present Status:
Silver Winds Church

Ishpeming

Butler Theatre
(Ishpeming)

City:
Ishpeming, Michigan

Address:
117-119 S. Main

Owner:
Edward Butler, Edward Wales

Built:
1915

Seating:
700

Film Release:
First Run

Present Status:
Converted in the 1980s adding second screen, closed 2001

Marquette

Nordic Theatre

City:
Marquette, Michigan

Address:
Washington at Main

Owner:
Delft Theatres

Built:
1936

Seating:
452

Film Release:
First Run

Present Status:
Renovated 1995 as Book World Bookstore

Marquette

Delft Theatre

City:
Marquette, Michigan

Address:
Main Street

Owner:
Delft Theatres

Built:
1914

Seating:
650

Film Release:
First Run

Present Status:
Remodeled in 1985 with second screen, sold to Rogers Cinema, Wisconsin

Sault Ste. Marie

Soo Theatre

City:
Sault Ste. Marie, Michigan

Address:
534 Ashmun

Owner:
Soo Amusement Co.,
Joseph C. DePaul

Built:
1930

Seating:
1,200

Film Release:
First Run

Present Status:
Converted in 1980s adding second screen, closed, for sale 2001.

Other Theatres

- Howell Theatre, Howell
- Regent Theatre, Allegan
- Garden, Frankfort

- Capitol Theatre, Owosso
- Creston Theatre, Grand Rapids
- Pines Theatre, Houghton Lake

• Oriole and Warfield theatres, Detroit

Photo Credits
and Bibliography

Photography Credits

Battle Creek Enquirer	Louanne Johnson Heidman
Bentley Library, University of Michigan	Manning Brothers Historical Collection
Butterfield Theatres Collection	Marquette County Historical Society
Delta County Historical Society	Michael V. Doyle Collection
Detroit Historical Museum	Michigan State University Archive and Historical Collections
Film Daily Yearbook	Michigan State University News
Flint Journal	Music Hall Archives
Flint Public Library	Neighborhood Cinema Group
Genesee County Historical Association	R.J. Hazen—MSU State News
GMI Historical Collection, Flint	Robert Jones, DDS
Goodrich Quality Theatres Inc.	Robinson Studios Collection
Grand Rapids Press	State of Michigan Archives
Grand Rapids Public Library	Strand Theatre Center Inc.
Jack Loeks Theatres Inc.	Thomas R. Kaekel
Jack R. Miller	View Two Plus/Michael M. Smith
Kalamazoo Gazette	Vince Doriean
Lansing State Journal	Western Michigan University Historical Collection
Lansing Public Library	William S. Davis
Leavenworth Photos, Lansing, Michigan	

Selected Bibliography

Anderson, Brett and Kalomirakis, Theo. *Private Theatres.* Harry Abrams, 1997.

Austin, Bruce A. *The Development and Decline of the Drive In Movie Theatre.* Economics and Law series, Albex, 1985.

Ayelsworth, Thomas and Virginia. *New York: The Glamour Years, 1919-1945.* Gallery, 1987.

Bowlers, David C. *Nickelodeon Theatres.* Vestal Press, 1986.

Carman, Beulali. *Looking Back: History of Houghton Lake.* 1979.

Chase, Linda. *Hollywood on Main Street, Movie House Paintings of Davis Cane.* Overlook Press, 1988.

Fuller, Kathyrn H. *At the Picture Show: Small Town Audiences and the Creation of Movie Fan Culture.* Smithsonian Institution Press, 1996.

Lowetine S. and Chappell L. *Marquette Then and Now.* North Shore Publications, 1999.

Grant, Michael. *In Trust of the Motion Picture.* University of California Press, 1960.

Margolies, John, and Gwathme, Emily. *Tickets to Paradise: American Movie Theatres and How We Had Fun.* Little Brown, 1991.

Naylor, David. *American Picture Palaces: Architecture of Fantasy.* Van Nostrund and Reinshold, 1981.

Olson, Gordon. *A Grand Rapids Sampler.* Grand Rapids Historical Association, 1992.

Pildas, Ave. *Movie Palaces.* Crown Publications, 1980.

Reddick, David, Bruce. *Movies Under the Stars: A History of the Drive In Theatre Industry 1933-1983.* Doctoral dissertation, Michigan State University, 1984.

Ribeilo, Steven, and Allen, Richard. *Reel Art: Great Posters from The Golden Age of the Silver Screen.* Abbevillre Press, 1988.

Russell, Hiliary. *Double Take.* Ontario Heritage Association , 1989.

Stanley, Robert. *The Celluloid Empire: A History of the American Industry.* Hasting House, 1978.

Stones, Barbara. *America Goes to the Movies: 100 Years of Motion Picture Exhibition.* National Theatre Owners, 1993.

Valentine, Maggie. *The Show Starts on the Sidewalk: Architectural History of the Movie Theatre.* S. Charles Lee, Yale University Press, 1994.

Wolicki, Dale Patrick. *The Historic Architecture of Bay City, Michigan.* Bay County Historical Society, 1998.

Index

Adams Theatre (Detroit) 28, 68
Advertising 37-45
Allendale Land Co. 6
Alpine Twin 15
AMC Theatres 24
American Seating Company 30
Ann Arbor 48-51
Ann Arbor Theater Company 6
Antitrust suit 1948 14
Arts Drive-In 15
Battle Creek 52-54
Bay City 56-59
Bay City (Colonial) Theatre 58
Bay State Theatre 30
Bay Theatre (State, Orpheum) 55-56
Beatty, Edward 6, 18
Beltline Drive-In 15
Berry, Earl 8-10
Bijou Theatre (Battle Creek) 4, 52-54
Bijou Theatrical Co. 6
Black Rose, The 43
Boone, Pat 8-10
Boshoven, Herbert R. 17-19
Butler Theatre 122
Butterfield & Johnson (B&J) Theatres Co. 6, 18-19, 30
Butterfield, Col. Walter Scott 3-10
Camp Custer 6
Campus (Lucon) Theatre (East Lansing) 110-111
Campus Theatre (Ann Arbor) 51
Capitol (Grand Circus) Theatre (Detroit) 29, 64
Capitol Theatre (Flint) 8-10, 27, 73-74
Capitol Theatre (Lansing) 105
Capitol Theatre (Owosso) 129
Celebration Cinemas 16
Center (Isis) Theatre vi, 5, 87
Cinerama (Wilson, Music Hall) Theatre 65
Colonial (Bay City) Theatre 58
Columbia (Savoy, Temple) Theatre 89
Consolidated Theatres Co. 5, 6
Crane, C. Howard 28-30, 55
Creston Theatre 129
Cross, Glenn A. 6
Delft Theatre 124
Della Theatre 78
Detroit 28, 59-71
Detroit Symphony Orchestra 29

Division Drive-In 15
Drive-Ins 13, 15, 23, 82
Duke Theatre (Detroit) 72
East Lansing-Lansing 102-112
Eastown Theatre vi, 18, 90
Ebel Construction Co. 30
Eberson, John 27, 73
Empire Theatre (Bay City) 57
Empress (Keith's, RKO) Theatre 5, 81, 84
Escanaba 121
Family Theatre vii
Finkel, Maurice 30
Fitzpatrick & McElroy Michigan Theatres 5
Flint 8-10, 73-80
Flint Capitol Theatre Co. 6
Flint Regent Theatre Co. 6
Fotonews (Powers) Theatre 14
Four-Star Theatre 18-19, 92
Fox Theatre 29, 60
Franklin Theatre 115, 117
Fuller Theatre 100
Garden (Rex) Theatre (Battle Creek) 6
Garden Theatre (Flint) 8-10, 80
Garden Theatre (Frankfort) 128
Geiger, Gary 24, 26
Gem Theatre (Detroit) 63
Getty Drive-In 15
Gladmer Theatre 104
Goodrich Quality Theatres 11-13, 26
Goodrich, Robert 12-13, 26
Goodrich, William "Emmett" 11-13
Grand Circus (Capitol) Theatre (Detroit) 29, 64
Grand Circus Park 28-30, 59
Grand Rapids vi, 5-6, 11-19, 31, 81-93
Grand Rapids Civic Theatre 13
Gull Lake Land Co. 6
Hamblin Opera House 4, 52-54
Hare, Michael 30
Harper Theatre 70
Heston, Charlton 8-10
Hollywood Theatre (Detroit) 71
Howell Theatre 128
IMAX Theatre 26
Irons, Harry 5
Ishpeming 122
Isis (Center) Theatre vi, 5, 87
Jackson 94-96
Johnson, Allen 6, 17-19, 30
Kalamazoo 97-101

Keefe, Walter 4
Keith-Albee circuit vi, 5
Keith's (RKO, Empress) Theatre 5, 31-32, 34, 81, 84
Kent (Orpheum) Theatre vi, 5, 88
Kunsky, John 28-29, 59
Lamb, Thomas 27
Lansing Arcade & Theatre Co. 6
Lansing Theatre 106
Lansing-East Lansing 40, 102-112
Little Studio Theatre 15
Loeks, Jack (Jim, John) 14-19, 26
Lucon Theatre (Campus) 110-111
Madison Theatre (Detroit) 28, 62
Majestic (Majestic Gardens) Theatre iv, 5, 13, 35, 85
Marquette 120, 123-124
Michigan (Strand) Theatre (Lansing) 36, 103
Michigan Street (Vogue) Theatre (Grand Rapids) 17
Michigan Theatre (Ann Arbor) 48-49
Michigan Theatre (Detroit) 28-30, 59, 67
Michigan Theatre (Escanaba) 121
Michigan Theatre (Flint) 79
Michigan Theatre (Jackson) 33, 95
Michigan Theatre (Kalamazoo) 99
Midtown Theatre vi, 15, 86
Miller, James Contracting 30
Music Hall (Wilson, Cinerama) Theatre 65
Muskegon 15
Neighborhood Cinema Group 24
Nordic Theatre 123
Norris, Walter 5
North Drive-In 15
Northtown Theatre (Lansing) 109
Northtown Theatre (Grand Rapids) 13
Oriental Theatre 29
Oriole Theatre 130
Orpheum (Kent) Theatre vi, 5, 88
Orpheum (State, Bay) Theatre (Bay City) 55-56
Orpheum Theatre (Lansing) 107
Osgood & Osgood 30
Our Theatre 18, 91
Palace Theatre (Flint) 76
Pillow Talk 45
Pines Theatre 129
Plainfield Drive-In 15
Plaza Theatre 108
Poisson family 17-19
Pontiac 113-114
Port Huron Family Theatre Co. 6
Post Theatre 6

Powers (Fotonews) Theatre 14
Prince of Foxes, The 41
Ramona Theatre 5
Rapp & Rapp 28
Redford Theatre 69
Regent Theatre (Allegan) 128
Regent Theatre (Flint) 75
Regent Theatre (Grand Rapids) 5-6, 81-83
Regent Theatre (Jackson) 96
Rex (Garden) Theatre 6
Reynolds, Howard T. 17
Rialto (Savoy, New Savoy, Royal) Theatre (Flint) 77
RKO (Keith's, Empress) Theatre (Grand Rapids) 5, 81, 84
Roosevelt Theatre (Grand Rapids) 18
Saginaw 115-117
Saginaw Franklin Theatre Co. 6
Sault Ste. Marie 125
Savoy (Temple, Columbia) Theatre 11-13, 89
Showcase Cinemas 24
"Siamese Byzantine" architecture 29
Snows of Kilimanjaro, The 44
Soo Theatre 125
Sound movies (early) 27-28
State (Bay, Orpheum) Theatre (Bay City) 55-56
State (Palms) Theatre (Detroit) 29, 61
State Theatre (Ann Arbor) 50
State Theatre (East Lansing) 112
State Theatre (Kalamazoo) 27, 98
Strand (Michigan) Theatre (Lansing) 36, 103
Strand Theatre (Grand Rapids) 5, 6
Strand Theatre (Pontiac) 113-114
Studio 28 Theatres 15
Temple (Savoy, Columbia) Theatre (Grand Rapids) 89
Temple Theatre (Saginaw) 115-116
Texas Carnival 42
United Artists Theatre 29, 66
Upper Peninsula 30, 119-125
Uptown Theatre 101
Varneau, Oscar 18
Vaudeville vi, 11, 53
Warfield Theatre 130
Wax Theatre 16
Wealthy Theatre 18-19, 93
Wilson (Cinerama, Music Hall) Theatre 65
Woodland Drive-In 15

Professor Michael Vincent Doyle, Ph.D., has spent thirty years at Michigan State University in East Lansing, Michigan. Doyle, a Grand Rapids native, has been a keen observer and collector of movie memorabilia for many years, amassing a large collection. He also is the author of *American West on Film: The Agrarian Frontier.*